Under Wraps

The Gift We Never Expected

Children's Leader Guide

Under Wraps
The Gift We Never Expected

Book
978-1-4267-9373-8
978-1-6308-8296-9 (Large Print)
Also available as an eBook

Leader Guide
978-1-4267-9375-2
Also available as an eBook

DVD
978-1-4267-9378-3

Devotional
978-1-4267-9376-9
Also available as an eBook

Children's Leader Guide
978-1-4267-9381-3

Youth Study Book
978-1-4267-9379-0
Also available as an eBook

Worship Planning
978-1-4267-9382-0 (Flash Drive)
978-1-6308-8069-9 (Download)

Under Wraps

The Gift We Never Expected

Jessica LaGrone

Andy Nixon

Rob Renfroe

Ed Robb

Children's Leader Guide
by Sally Hoelscher

Abingdon Press
Nashville

UNDER WRAPS: THE GIFT WE NEVER EXPECTED

Children's Leader Guide
by Sally Hoelscher

Copyright © 2014 Abingdon Press

All rights reserved.

This book is printed on acid-free, elemental chlorine-free paper.

ISBN 978-1-4267-9381-3

14 15 16 17 18 19 20 21 22 23—10 9 8 7 6 5 4 3 2 1
MANUFACTURED IN THE UNITED STATES OF AMERICA

Contents

Under Wraps activity center   *Photo courtesy of The Woodlands UMC*

To the Leader

This children's leader guide is designed for use with the churchwide Advent program *Under Wraps: The Gift We Never Expected* by Jessica LaGrone, Andy Nixon, Rob Renfroe, and Ed Robb. This guide includes five lessons—a lesson for each Sunday in Advent and a Christmas lesson.

Under Wraps, the theme of this study, presents Advent as a time of preparation to remember the greatest gift ever given—Jesus. Talking with children about Jesus as a gift from God puts the birth of Jesus into language they can understand. Children speak the language of gift giving and receiving.

Every child (and, if we're honest, every adult) likes presents. Receiving gifts is fun—the anticipation, the surprise. Giving presents is fun too. Choosing a gift for someone and watching their reaction as they open it provides a special kind of joy. Children can understand that God chose to send the gift of Jesus to the world because God knew Jesus was exactly what the world needed. During Advent we prepare once again to thank God for the best gift of all.

Lesson Plan Format

The lessons in this guide, designed for children five to eleven years old, are presented in a large group/small group format. Children begin with time spent at activity centers, followed by time together as a large group. Children end the lesson in small groups determined by age. Each lesson plan contains the following sections:

Focus for the Teacher

The information in this section will provide you with background information about the week's lesson. Use this section for your own study as you prepare.

Explore Interest Groups

You'll find in this section ideas for a variety of activity centers. The activities will prepare the children to hear the Bible story. Allow the children to choose one or more of the activities that interest them. Occasionally there will be an activity that is recommended for all children, usually because it relates directly to a later activity. When this is the case, it will be noted in the sidebar notes.

Large Group

The children will come together as a large group to hear the story for the week. This section begins with a transition activity followed by the story and a Bible verse activity. A worship time concludes the large-group time.

Small Groups

Children are divided into age-level groups for small-group time. Depending on the size of your class, you may need to have more than one group for each age level. It is recommended that each small group contain no more than ten children.

Young Children

The activities in this section are designed for children five to seven years old.

Older Children

The activities in this section are designed for children eight to eleven years old.

Reproducible Pages

At the end of each lesson are reproducible pages, to be photocopied and handed out for all the children to use during that lesson's activities.

Schedule

Many churches have weeknight programs that include an evening meal; an intergenerational gathering time; and classes for children, youth, and adults. The following schedule illustrates one way to organize a weeknight program.

5:30	Meal
6:00	Intergenerational gathering introducing weekly themes and places for the lesson. This time may include presentations, skits, music, and opening or closing prayers.
6:15–8:15	Classes for children, youth, and adults.

Churches may want to do this study as a Sunday school program. This setting would be similar to the weeknight setting. The following schedule takes into account a shorter class time, which is the norm for Sunday morning programs.

10 minutes	Intergenerational gathering
45 minutes	Classes for children, youth, and adults

Choose a schedule that works best for your congregation and its Christian education programs.

Blessings to you and the children as you prepare to celebrate the birth of Jesus.

1 Waiting for God

Objectives

The children will
- hear Isaiah 9:6-7.
- discover that Isaiah foretold Jesus' birth many years before it happened.
- learn that people waited a long time for Jesus to be born.
- explore the idea of waiting for God in their lives.

Theme

Isaiah spoke words of hope to a weary world.

Bible Verse

A child is born to us, a son is given to us. (Isaiah 9:6a)

Focus for the Teacher

Isaiah's message of a promised Messiah was delivered to people who were in need of just such a message of hope. Isaiah lived about 500 years after God had delivered the Israelites from slavery in Egypt. Many of the Israelite people had failed to put their trust in God and had begun worshiping other gods. The people were looking to alliances with other countries to protect them instead of putting their trust in God. This was a time of social injustice, exploitation of the poor, and corruption of political and religious leaders. Does this sound familiar? Many of the issues facing the Israelites are ones we continue to struggle with today.

Isaiah warned the people of Israel that they needed to repent of their wrongdoing and put their trust, once again, in God. Amidst the warnings, in the ninth chapter of Isaiah we find a message of hope—God would send a Savior. Isaiah's description of peaceful times ahead brought hope to a weary world. Although our world is much different from when Isaiah lived,

> Christmas is an exciting time to teach children.

we still long for the peace Isaiah foretold. We still need hope.

In Isaiah 9:6, the attributes of the promised Savior are described. The coming Messiah would be the ideal king, representing the best qualities of Israel's past kings. He would be a wise leader (Wonderful Counselor). He would be powerful (Mighty God). He would display fatherly love and care (Everlasting Father). He would bring peace and prosperity (Prince of Peace).

Christmas is an exciting time to teach children. The Christmas story is a familiar one to most children. Children like hearing the Christmas story, and they enjoy celebrating Christmas. When given encouragement and opportunity, children are very generous and like to be helpers. As you teach, let the enthusiasm of the children remind you that we have much to celebrate.

Explore Interest Groups

Be sure that adult leaders are waiting when the first child arrives. Greet and welcome the children. Get the children involved in an activity that interests them and introduces the theme for the day's activities.

Prepare the Large Group Area

- **Say:** Today is the first of four Sundays of Advent. Advent is a time before Christmas when we get ready to celebrate the birth of Jesus. Sometimes we keep track of the Sundays of Advent by lighting candles on an Advent wreath. We are going to make an Advent wreath using presents instead of candles. The presents will remind us that God sent Jesus as a gift to the world.

- Divide children into five groups and give each group a box.

- Give three groups purple paper, one group pink paper, and one group white paper.

- Encourage each group of children to work together to cover their box by tearing the paper they have been given into smaller pieces and gluing the pieces onto the box. Have the children overlap the torn pieces of paper in order to cover the entire box.

- Once the boxes have been covered, have the children place them in the front of the large-group area. Arrange the purple and pink presents in a circle and place the white present in the center of the circle.

- **Say:** We will use this Advent wreath during our large-group time all month.

Prepare

- ✓ Provide five large cardboard boxes, glue, and construction paper in the following colors: purple, pink, and white

- ✓ Note: The boxes can be any size and do not need to be all the same size.

- ✓ Note: Some of the activities throughout this study refer to the Sundays of Advent. If you use the study for a midweek program, refer to the week of Advent instead of the Sunday.

Prepare

✓ Provide copies of **Reproducible 1a: Scroll Ornament**, found at the end of the lesson.

✓ Provide plastic straws, colored pencils, scissors, glue, and ribbon.

✓ Use fancy wrapping paper and ribbon to decorate a large box with a lid, wrapping the lid separately so the box can be opened without tearing the paper. Place wrapping paper, gift tags, and tape in the decorated box.

✓ Note: This wrapped box will be used for Lessons 1 through 4. You may choose to fill the box with a different kind of wrapping paper each week.

Make a Scroll Ornament

- **Say:** When we exchange gifts at Christmas time, we remember that God gave us the greatest gift of all by sending Jesus into the world. Let's see what is in this present.

- Have the children help you open the box to find the wrapping supplies.

- **Ask:** What do you think you could do with this gift? (Wrap presents)

- **Say:** Today you are going to make two ornaments. One ornament will be for you to keep, and one will be for you to give away to someone. After the ornaments are made, you can wrap one of them to give to someone else.

- Give each child a copy of the Scroll Ornament page.

- Invite a child to read the Bible verse on the ornament aloud.

- **Say:** Our Bible story today is about the prophet Isaiah delivering a message of hope to God's people. This Bible verse is part of Isaiah's hopeful message.

- **Ask:** Who do you think the child in this verse is? (Hint: We are preparing to celebrate his birth: Jesus.)

- Have each child cut out the scroll ornaments.

- Have each child cut four pieces of straw about 3 inches in length.

- Encourage each child to wrap each short end of the cutout ornaments around a straw piece and glue it in place, rolling the paper toward the writing on the ornament so the finished ornaments resemble scrolls.

- Have each child cut two pieces of ribbon approximately 6 inches long. Have them tie one end of a piece of ribbon to each end of the straw piece at the top of one ornament to form a hanging loop, and then repeat with the other ornament and piece of ribbon.

- Invite each child to use colored pencils to decorate their ornaments.

- **Say:** Think about whom you would like to give your second ornament to.

- Help each child wrap one of their ornaments to be given as a gift.

Names for Jesus Word Find

- Give each child a copy of the "Names for Jesus Word Find" and a pencil.

- Encourage each child to find the hidden words.

- **Ask:** What do all these words have in common? (They are all names sometimes used to describe Jesus.)

Prepare

✓ Provide pencils and copies of **Reproducible 1b: Names for Jesus Word Find**, found at the end of this lesson.

Answer Key

```
K M B N E T R O X A Z P L M V B J E
U N C W R C H I L D D O E T E E Y E
N T I D H A D V U Y W R T I O V U Y
G J L P I O E F C O U W E N D E V T
V E V E W C P R I M S D R P M R D I
W O N D E R F U L C O U N S E L O R
J Y T U P R W I V C D G A S Z A G O
H U R E N S D P I Y K L L E R S Y H
G Y T R W P U V M B X S F O U T T T
E S U G O D I S W I T H A S S I H U
G E V S P O H K E L M D T A I N G A
I H N I E R V B N J I S H N X G I L
G H T O M M A E C E A P E G N F M I
K E C A E P F O E C N I R P N A C R
R W P K G L L M I B N V T Y R T W R
```

The Waiting Game

- Have all of the children except one sit in a circle facing one another.

- Have the remaining child walk around the outside of the circle, gently tapping each child on the head and saying, "Wait."

- After tapping several children on the head, have the tapper choose one child and say, "Go!" as they tap that child.

- Have the second child jump up and chase the first child around the circle as the first child tries to get back to the empty spot.

- If the second child tags the first child, have the first child continue tapping and saying, "Wait, wait, wait . . . go!"

- If the first child is successful in reaching the empty space, have the second child become the tapper.

- **Ask:** How do you feel when you're waiting to find out if you will be the one chosen to jump up? Is it hard to wait?

- **Say:** Our Bible story today is about waiting.

Large Group

Bring all the children together to experience the Bible story. Use a bell to alert the children to the large-group time.

How Long Must We Wait?

- Have the children sit in the large-group area where they cannot see a clock.

- **Say:** We are going to play a game. I am going to say, "Start," and then after awhile I will say, "Stop." After I say, "Stop," I want you to guess how long it has been since I said "Start."

- Play the game several times, gradually increasing the time before you say "Stop."

- After each round, let the children guess how long the time was before you tell them.

- **Ask:** Was it hard for you to wait until I said "Stop"?

- **Say:** You only had to wait seconds until I said "Stop," but in our Bible story today we will hear about God's people waiting 700 years for a leader God promised to send.

Prepare

✓ Provide copies of **Reproducible 1c: Waiting for God: Isaiah's Prophecy**, found at the end of this lesson.

✓ Provide Bibles.

Waiting for God: Isaiah's Prophecy

- **Say:** Today is the first Sunday of Advent. Advent is a time of preparation and waiting.

- **Ask:** What are we waiting for during Advent? (Christmas) What do we celebrate at Christmas? (The birth of Jesus)

- **Say:** Today's Bible story is about a man who told people about Jesus a long time before Jesus was born.

- Have the children find the book of Isaiah in their Bibles.

- **Ask:** Is Isaiah in the Old Testament or New Testament? (Old Testament) Was Isaiah written before or after Jesus was born? (Before)

- Invite a confident reader to help you read the story.

- Read the Bible story from "Waiting for God: Isaiah's Prophecy," having your volunteer read the words in bold type.

- Thank your volunteer for helping you tell the story.

- **Ask:** What is a prophet? (One who delivers messages from God.) Why were God's people in need of hope? (They were not happy. People were being treated unfairly.) How long is Advent? (Four weeks)

- **Say:** Imagine if you had to wait 700 years for Christmas instead of four weeks!

- **Ask:** How do you think the people felt when they were waiting such a long time for the promised to be born? (Discouraged, tired of waiting, impatient) Do you think some people might have forgotten what they were waiting for? How is Isaiah's message a message of hope? (It promises that things will be better someday.)

- **Say:** Even though they had to wait a long time, the people kept waiting and hoping because they knew that God had promised a Savior, and God keeps promises.

Bible Verse in Two Parts

- Show the children the Bible verse.

- Encourage the children to read the verse with you.

- Divide the class into four groups and assign each group a number, 1 through 4.

- **Say:** Now we are going to divide our verse into two parts. The first part will be "A child is born to us." The second part will be "A son is given to us." I am going to say two numbers. The first number will indicate which group will say the first part of the verse, and the second number will indicate which group will say the second part of the verse. For example, if I said 3-1, group 3 would say, "A child is born to us," and group 1 would say, "A son is given to us." Pay attention so you know when it is your group's turn.

- Say various number combinations, allowing the groups time to say the verse after each combination.

- **Ask:** Who is the child Isaiah predicted would be born? (Jesus)

Prepare

✓ Write the Bible verse on a marker board or a piece of mural paper and place it where it can easily be seen. (A child is born to us, a son is given to us. Isaiah 9:6a)

Prepare

✓ On separate pieces of paper, write: Hope, Peace, Joy, Love, Jesus

✓ Place each of the words in one of the boxes of the Advent wreath the children made earlier in the lesson. The word *Jesus* will go in the white box. The word *Joy* will go in the pink box. Mark the boxes in some way so you know what word is in each box.

✓ Provide tape to attach the word to the outside of the box.

✓ Decorate a large poster to resemble a wrapped present (or wrap a very large box.) On the poster or large box place a large gift tag that reads: "Christmas Under Wraps: Advent." Place the poster or box near the Advent wreath.

Hoping and Waiting

• **Say:** Earlier, some of you helped to make an Advent wreath with presents instead of candles. As we prepare to celebrate Christmas, we remember that God gave the first Christmas present ever—Jesus. Today is the first Sunday of Advent, so we will open the first present.

• Invite a child to open the purple box containing the word *Hope*. Show the class what is inside. Tape the word *Hope* to the outside of the box.

• **Say:** Today we unwrap and receive the gift of hope.

• Lead the children in the following cheer:
  Leader: Give me an H!
  Children: H!
  Leader: Give me an O!
  Children: O!
  Leader: Give me a P!
  Children: P!
  Leader: Give me an E!
  Children: E!
  Leader: What's that spell?
  Children: Hope!
  Leader: One more time!
  Children: Hope!

• **Say:** The word *Hope* reminds us of Isaiah's message of hope for God's people many years before Jesus was born.

• **Ask:** What is the difference between a hope and a wish?

• **Say:** When you make a wish, you want something and you know that you may or may not receive it. When you have hope, you believe that someday the thing you are hoping for will happen. God's people had to wait a long time for Jesus to be born, but they continued to hope and believe that God would send them a new leader.

• **Say:** Today we are going to learn a breath prayer. As we pray, we will take slow breaths in and out. As we breathe in, I will say, "God of Hope," and as we breathe out, I will say, "Be with us as we wait." I will say the prayer three times.

• Have the children breathe in and out slowly while you pray.

• **Say:** During the next week, if there are times when it feels hard to wait for Christmas, stop and say this breath prayer to yourself.

• Dismiss children to their small groups.

Small Groups

Divide the children into small groups. You may organize the groups around age levels or around readers and non-readers. Keep the groups small, with a maximum of ten children in each group. You may need to have more than one group of each age level.

Young Children (Ages 5–7)

- **Ask:** What are we waiting for during Advent? (Christmas) What do we celebrate at Christmas? (The birth of Jesus)

- **Say:** The people who lived during Isaiah's time were waiting also. At that time not everyone was happy. Some countries were at war. Some people were treated unfairly. Not everyone had a place to live and enough food to eat. People were hoping that someday things would be better.

- **Ask:** Do people today still hope for things to get better?

- **Say:** Isaiah told the people that one day a wise, powerful, caring leader would come and show them how to live in peace. God's people hoped that Isaiah was right.

- **Ask:** Was Isaiah right? Who was the leader?

- **Say:** Jesus was the leader people hoped for. During his lifetime he showed people how to live and taught people about the way God wanted them to live.

- Give each child a piece of paper.

- Have children use crayons to trace around one of their hands on the piece of paper. Encourage children to help each other with tracing.

- Have children write their names on the palms of their handprints.

- **Ask:** What are some things Jesus taught about how we are to live? (Keep God first, love one another, be kind, care for people in need, and much more!)

- Allow children to share their ideas.

- Encourage children to write one thing they can do to follow Jesus' teaching on each finger and thumb on their papers.

- **Say:** Unlike the people at the time Isaiah lived, we don't have to wait for Jesus to be born. As we celebrate Jesus' birth, we can follow Jesus' teachings and do our part to make the world a better place. Take your handprints home to remind you to follow Jesus while you wait.

- **Pray:** God of Hope, thank you for Jesus. Help us to follow his teachings and share your love with others while we wait to once again celebrate Jesus' birth. Amen.

Prepare

✓ Provide paper and crayons

Prepare

✓ Provide paper, scissors, and pencils.

✓ Note: Be sure to try the activity in advance to so you can help the children.

Older Children (Ages 8–11)

- **Say:** At the time Isaiah lived, people were hoping for a wise, powerful, caring leader to come and show them how to live in peace. Jesus was that leader. Every year we wait to celebrate Jesus' birth, but we don't have to wait for Christmas to follow Jesus' teachings.

- **Ask:** What did Jesus teach about how we are to live? (Keep God first, love one another, be kind, care for people in need, and much more!)

- **Say:** When we follow the teachings of Jesus, we help make the world a better place.

- **Ask:** What are some things you can do, either yourself or with your family or friends, to help make the world a better place?

- Allow children an opportunity to offer their thoughts and ideas.

- **Say:** You are going to make a small book of ideas about things you can do to make the world a better place while you are waiting to celebrate Christmas.

- Give each child a piece of paper and have them make a small book using the following directions.
    1. Fold the paper in half bringing the long sides together, crease the fold, and then unfold the paper.
    2. Fold the paper in half bringing the short sides together, crease the fold, and then unfold the paper.
    3. Fold each short edge in to meet the centerfold line, crease the folds, and then unfold the paper.
    4. Refold the paper in half bringing the short sides together.
    5. Cutting along the fold line and beginning at the folded edge, cut halfway across the page. Note that another fold line marks the halfway point.
    6. Unfold the paper and refold it in half bringing the long edges together.
    7. Holding one short edge in each hand and the cut section at the top, push your hands together so the middle sections fold out and the paper can then be folded to form a small book.

- Have each child write the following words on the front of the book: *While I wait, I can…*

- Encourage children to write something on each page of the book describing what they can do to make the world a better place.

- **Say:** Take your book home as a reminder, and see how many of these things you can do before Christmas. Invite your family to join with you in doing good while you wait.

- **Pray:** God of Hope, thank you for the gift of Jesus, who taught us how to make the world a better place. As we wait to celebrate Jesus' birth, help us remember to keep following Jesus' teachings. Amen.

Under Wraps: Children's Leader Guide

Scroll Ornament

A child is
born to us,
a son is
given to us.
(Isaiah 9:6a)

A child is
born to us,
a son is
given to us.
(Isaiah 9:6a)

Names for Jesus Word Find

Find the following words hidden in the puzzle below. Words may be backwards, horizontal, vertical, or diagonal.

ETERNAL FATHER

JESUS

MIGHTY GOD

PRINCE OF PEACE

WONDERFUL COUNSELOR

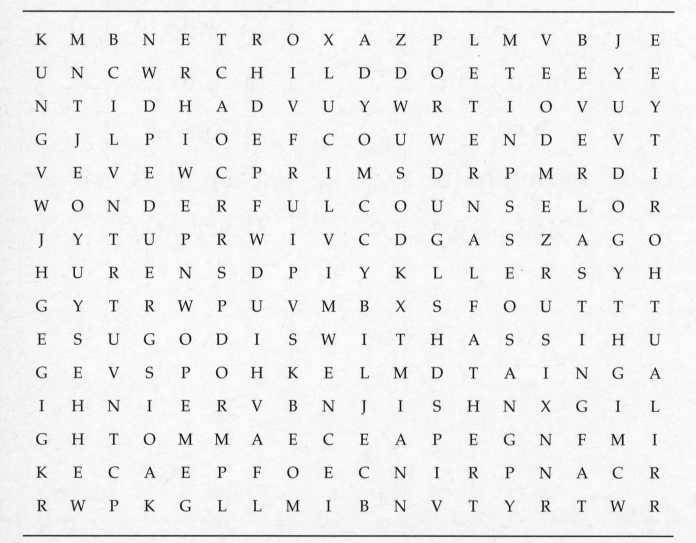

K M B N E T R O X A Z P L M V B J E
U N C W R C H I L D D O E T E E Y E
N T I D H A D V U Y W R T I O V U Y
G J L P I O E F C O U W E N D E V T
V E V E W C P R I M S D R P M R D I
W O N D E R F U L C O U N S E L O R
J Y T U P R W I V C D G A S Z A G O
H U R E N S D P I Y K L L E R S Y H
G Y T R W P U V M B X S F O U T T T
E S U G O D I S W I T H A S S I H U
G E V S P O H K E L M D T A I N G A
I H N I E R V B N J I S H N X G I L
G H T O M M A E C E A P E G N F M I
K E C A E P F O E C N I R P N A C R
R W P K G L L M I B N V T Y R T W R

Waiting for God: Isaiah's Prophecy

Isaiah was a prophet who lived over 700 years before Jesus was born. A prophet is a person who speaks for God. Isaiah delivered many messages from God.

At the time Isaiah lived, God's people were unhappy. Some people had forgotten that God is the only true God and had begun to worship other gods. Many people were being treated unfairly. Isaiah delivered messages that warned people they needed to recognize the things they were doing wrong and to do better. Isaiah also delivered messages of hope that in the future, life would be better.

Listen to one of Isaiah's messages of hope. Isaiah said that one day these things would happen.

> A child is born to us, a son is given to us,
> and authority will be on his shoulders.
> He will be named
> Wonderful Counselor, Mighty God,
> Eternal Father, Prince of Peace.

In other words, one day a child will be born who will be the reason to celebrate. He will be a wise, powerful, and caring leader who will bring peace.

> There will be vast authority
> and endless peace
> for David's throne and for his kingdom,
> establishing and sustaining it
> with justice and righteousness
> now and forever.
> The zeal of the LORD of heavenly forces will do this.

In other words, the descendants of David will live in peace. People will be treated justly and fairly. God is sending the one who will lead the people into this new way of living.

Based on Isaiah 9:6-7

2 Surprised by God

Objectives	Theme
The children will • hear Luke 1:26-38. • discover that God sent Gabriel to tell Mary she was going to have a baby. • learn that Mary was surprised by the news that she was to be the mother of the Messiah. • explore the idea of being surprised by God in their lives.	God's ways can be surprising. **Bible Verse** "Don't be afraid, Mary. God is honoring you." (Luke 1:30b)

Focus for the Teacher

"Don't be afraid." The New Testament contains five accounts of angels speaking these words. Three of these accounts are connected with announcements of Jesus' birth: to Joseph (Matthew 1:20), to Mary (Luke 1:30), and to the shepherds (Luke 2:10). The other two occurrences are found in the announcement of John the Baptist's upcoming birth to Zechariah (Luke 1:13) and in the reassurance to the women at the empty tomb following Jesus' resurrection (Matthew 28:5). The frequency with which angels spoke the reassuring phrase "Don't be afraid" makes one wonder why it was necessary! Were angels terrifying to behold, such that their appearance required reassurance? Or did the appearance of an angel usually signify such an important pronouncement, and possibly a life-altering event, that their presence automatically elicited a response of fear?

For Mary, her encounter with the angel Gabriel certainly qualified as a surprising and life-changing event. Life as she knew it was about to change dramatically. Had she known how much,

> God is at work among ordinary people.

she might have been even more afraid. Encounters with angels are not something one can plan for.

Mary was a young girl, probably twelve or thirteen years old. This was the age at which girls were married during Bible times. She was engaged to Joseph, an arrangement likely made by her father, but they were not yet married. Mary was not a queen or a princess, but simply a young girl engaged to be married to a carpenter. Mary lived in a small town, Nazareth in Galilee, which was never mentioned in the Old Testament. She was an ordinary girl in an insignificant town.

The angel told Mary that she had found favor with God. Many assumed that those blessed by God would enjoy wealth and good health. Mary's blessing, however, was that she would have a child out of wedlock. Mary's response of "How can this be?" seems appropriate and believable. The angel assures her that it is true, and that the baby is God's son. God is at work among ordinary people, choosing to send Jesus as a message of God's love, in a surprising, unexpected, and unconventional way.

Explore Interest Groups

Be sure that adult leaders are waiting when the first child arrives. Greet and welcome the children. Get the children involved in an activity that interests them and introduces the theme for the day's activities.

Make an Angel Ornament

- Show the children the wrapped box.

- **Ask:** Do you remember who gave the first Christmas present? (God) And what was the present? (Jesus)

- Have the children help you open the wrapped box.

- **Say:** Our Bible story today is about the angel Gabriel delivering a message to Mary. Today you are going to make angel ornaments. As you did last week, you will make two ornaments, one to keep and one to give away to someone. When your ornaments are made, you may use the supplies in this box to wrap one of them.

- Give each child two copies of the Angel Ornament Patterns.

- Encourage each child to make two ornaments, following these directions to make each one:

- Cut out the three circles and one oval shape along the solid lines.

- Cut along the dotted lines to cut the medium-sized circle in half and to cut out the middle section of the oval.
  - o Take the largest circle and fold it into an upside-down cone shape by choosing any point on the edge of the circle and folding the edges on either side of that point toward the center until they are just touching. This is the angel's body.
  - o Glue the smallest circle on the top of the upside-down cone, covering about 1/2-inch of the point. This circle is the angel's head.
  - o Glue the two half-circles to the back of the angel's body to form wings. The flat edge of the half-circles should be up, and the half-circles will just overlap behind the angel's head.
  - o Glue the oval ring on the angel's head to form a halo.
  - o Cut a piece of ribbon about six inches long, tie the ends together to form a hanging loop, and secure the hanging loop to the back of the angel with a small piece of tape.

- Invite the children to use crayons to decorate their angel ornaments.

- Encourage the children to decide whom they will give their second ornaments to.

- Have the children wrap one of their ornaments.

- **Say:** When you give this present to someone, tell him or her about the Christmas present God gave to the world.

Prepare

- ✓ Provide copies on card-stock of **Reproducible 2a: Angel Ornament Patterns**, found at the end of this lesson. You will need two copies for each child.

- ✓ Provide crayons, scissors, glue, transparent tape, and ribbon.

- ✓ Use the wrapped box prepared for Lesson 1 filled with gift-wrapping supplies. You may choose to add new wrapping paper to the box.

Surprised by God

Prepare

✓ Provide a pitcher of water, a plastic zippered bag, a shallow baking pan or container for catching water, a sharpened pencil, paper cups, ping-pong balls, toothpicks, dish soap, and paper towels.

✓ Fill the plastic bag about two-thirds full of water and close it tightly.

Surprising Science

- **Say:** Today we are going to do some experiments with water.

- Show the children the plastic bag you have filled with water and the sharpened pencil.

- **Ask:** What will happen if I poke this bag with this pencil?

- Holding the bag over the shallow container (just in case), poke the pencil through one side of the bag and out of the other side, through the water, leaving the pencil sticking through the bag.

- **Ask:** What happened? (Hopefully, no water spilled out because the plastic bag formed a seal around the pencil as it was poked through.) Did this surprise you? What will happen if I remove the pencil?
(The water will spill out of the holes left in the bag.)

- Remove the pencil and allow the water to flow into the shallow container. Add more water to the pan if necessary so the water is about an inch deep.

- Show the children two toothpicks.

- **Ask:** Will toothpicks float or sink? (They will float because wood is less dense than water.)

- Place the two toothpicks on top of the water at one end of the container, overlapping the ends of the toothpicks to form an arrow pointing to the other end of the container.

- Take a third toothpick and dip it in dishwashing liquid.

- **Ask:** What do you think will happen if I dip this toothpick in this pan of water?

- Dip the soap-covered end of the toothpick inside the "V" formed by the two toothpicks. The two toothpicks should move to the other end of the container, possibly also moving away from each other. This is a result of the soap interfering with the surface tension of the water.

- **Ask:** Was this what you expected to happen or did it surprise you?

- Divide the children into small groups.

- Give each group a paper cup and a ping-pong ball.

- Have each group pour some water into their cup.

- Challenge each group to balance the ball on top of the water in the center of the cup so it does not touch the sides.

- **Ask:** Does it surprise you that you can't get the ball to stay in the center of the cup? Do you think it can be done?

- Pour additional water into each group's cup so that each cup is full and almost overflowing.

- Once again challenge each group to balance the ball on top of the water in the center of the cup so it does not touch the sides of the cup. This time the ball should stay away from the edges.

- **Say:** Sometimes things that happen surprise us. In our Bible story today we will hear about some big surprises!

You've Been Chosen Tag

- **Say:** We are going to play a game of tag. We will start with one person being "It" and end with everyone being "It." The person who is "It" will tag someone who will then join hands with them and become part of "It." While continuing to hold hands, one of them will tag someone else who will then join hands with them and become part of "It." The only other rule is that every time "It" tags someone, they must shout, "You've been chosen!"

- Choose a child to begin the game.

- Play the game. When every child has been chosen, choose a new child to start the game and let the children play again.

- **Say:** During our Bible story today we will hear of someone being chosen for a very important job.

Prepare

✓ Identify a large open area free of obstacles to play this game.

Large Group

Bring all the children together to experience the Bible story. Use a bell to alert the children to the large-group time.

Surprising Directions

- Have the children stand up.

- **Say:** I am going to give you some directions to follow. You'll want to listen closely, because these directions may surprise you.

- Give the following directions, pausing momentarily where indicated by the ellipses. (. . .)
    - o Clap . . . your elbows together.
    - o Turn around . . . your hands.
    - o Stomp . . . your fist on the ground.
    - o Snap . . . to attention and stand up tall.
    - o March . . . your fingers up your arm.
    - o Hop . . . to it and have a seat.

Prepare

✓ Provide copies of **Reproducible 2b: Surprised by God: Gabriel Visits Mary**, found at the end of this lesson, for each child to take home.

✓ Use a marker to write the word "Surprise!" on a piece of paper.

Surprised by God: Gabriel Visits Mary

- **Say:** I need your help telling the Bible story today.

- Show the children the paper that says "Surprise!"

- **Say:** At certain times during the story I am going to hold up this piece of paper. When I do, that's your cue to shout, "Surprise!" Let's practice.

- Hold up the sign and encourage the children to shout, "Surprise!"

- Read the Bible story from "Surprised by God: Gabriel Visits Mary," holding up the sign and encouraging the children to respond where indicated in the story.

- **Ask:** What were the four surprises in our story? (An angel, news that Mary was pregnant, the baby was God's son, Elizabeth was pregnant) Do you think Mary was planning on having God's son?

- **Say:** Life doesn't always go the way we plan, does it? Sometimes surprising things happen. Sometimes those surprises are good things, and sometimes they are challenging things. Mary was able to accept Gabriel's news when she remembered God would be with her. God is with us too no matter what surprises we get.

Under Wraps: Children's Leader Guide

Volume Control

- Show the children the Bible verse.

- Invite the children to read the verse with you.

- **Ask:** Why do you think Mary was afraid when Gabriel came to visit her? (It's not every day an angel comes to visit.)

- **Say:** Now let's pretend that I am a volume control slider. We will sign and say the verse together three more times. When I am standing over here (move all the way to your right side) the volume needs to be very soft. As I walk across the room, the volume increases. And when I am standing over here (move all the way to your left side) the volume is very loud.

- Encourage the children to say the verse with you three more times as you control the volume with your position.

Prepare

✓ Write the Bible verse on a marker board or a piece of mural paper and place it where it can easily be seen. ("Don't be afraid, Mary. God is honoring you." Luke 1:30b)

Surprised and Peaceful

- **Say:** Last week some of you helped make an Advent wreath for us that has presents instead of candles.

- **Ask:** What word did we find in the first present last week? (*Hope*)

- **Say:** Today we will open a second box.

- Invite a child to open the purple present containing the word *Peace* and show the class what is inside. Tape the word *Peace* to the outside of the box.

- **Say:** Today we unwrap and receive the gift of peace.

- Lead the children in the following cheer:

  Leader: Give me an P!
  Children: P!

  Leader: Give me an E!
  Children: E!

  Leader: Give me a A!
  Children: A!

  Leader: Give me an C!
  Children: C!

Prepare

✓ Provide tape to attach the word to the outside of the box.

Leader: Give me an E!
Children: E!

Leader: What's that spell?
Children: Peace!

Leader: One more time!
Children: Peace!

- **Say:** The word *Peace* reminds us that even when life surprises us, we can find peace knowing that God is with us. Gabriel surprised Mary with the news that she was going to have God's son. Mary might have been surprised at first, but then she remembered that God would be with her.

- **Say:** Today we are going to learn another breath prayer. As we pray, we will take slow breaths in and out. As we breathe in, I will say, "God of Peace," and as we breathe out, I will say, "Be with us always." I will say the prayer three times.

- Have the children breathe in and out slowly while you pray.

- **Say:** During the next week if there are times when you need life to be more peaceful, stop and say this breath prayer to yourself.

- Dismiss children to their small groups.

Small Groups

Divide the children into small groups. You may organize the groups around age levels or around readers and nonreaders. Keep the groups small, with a maximum of ten children in each group. You may need to have more than one group of each age level.

Young Children (Ages 5–7)

- Have the children sit in a circle.

- **Ask:** If you have a message for someone, what are some ways you might get it to him or her?

- **Say:** Today we are going to pass some messages around our circle.

- Whisper a message to one child.

- Have the child whisper the message to the child sitting next to him or her.

- Have each child pass along the message when they receive it by whispering it to the next child.

- When the message has gone all the way around the circle, have the last child say the message out loud.

- Compare the ending message with the beginning message.

- Play the game several times with different messages and beginning with different children.

- **Ask:** How did God deliver a message to Mary? (God sent an angel.) How do you think Mary felt when she saw an angel? How would you feel if an angel suddenly appeared to you? What was Mary's response to the angel's news? (She agreed to do what God wanted her to do.) Do you think you would have agreed so quickly?

- **Say:** Let's review our Bible story. We will go around the circle, and each person will share one thing they remember about the story. Try to say something that has not already been said. The story does not have to be in order.

- Encourage the children to share what they remember. If necessary, ask questions to help them remember the story.

- Invite children to remember a time when something surprising happened in their lives. Children do not need to share what the surprising event was unless they would like to, but invite them to share how they felt at the time.

- **Say:** No matter what happens in our lives, we can remember, as Mary did, that God is with us. God will be with us during good surprises and challenging surprises.

- Have the children stand in a circle.

Prepare

- Plan some messages to use for the game. Possible messages include:
  - God sent Jesus because God loves us.
  - An angel told Mary she would have a baby boy and she would not name him Joseph.
  - Mary was engaged to be married to Joseph, but she was still living in her father's house.

- Have the children spread their feet apart so the each child's feet are against the feet of the children on each side of them.
- **Pray:** God of Peace, thank you for your presence in our lives. As we continue to prepare and wait for Christmas, we celebrate your love for us. Amen.

Prepare

✓ Provide a copy for each child of **Reproducible 2b: Surprised by God: Gabriel Visits Mary**, found at the end of this lesson.

✓ Provide a beanbag.

✓ Note: If you do not have a beanbag, use a clean sock rolled into a ball.

Older Children (Ages 8–11)

- Have the children sit in a circle.
- Give the beanbag to one of the children.
- **Say:** Let's review our Bible story today. When you have the beanbag, share one thing you remember about the story. Try to say something that has not already been said. The story does not have to be in order. After you have shared, gently toss the beanbag to someone else in the circle.
- Encourage the children to share what they remember. If necessary, ask questions to help them remember the story.
- Give each child a copy of "Surprised by God: Gabriel Visits Mary."
- **Say:** We are going to take another look at our story, but this time we are going to play the "What if . . .?" game. The person holding the beanbag will look at the story and come up with a question that begins with the phrase, "What if . . ." For example, "What if Gabriel refused to deliver God's message?" or "What if Mary had said she didn't want to have God's baby?" The rest of us will use our imaginations to answer the question and say what might have happened if things had occurred differently. After we've answered the question, the beanbag will be gently tossed to someone else who will ask us a "What if . . ." question.
- Encourage the children to ask "What if . . ." questions and to use their imaginations to answer the questions.
- Invite children to remember a time when something surprising happened in their lives.
- **Say:** No matter what happens in our lives, we can remember, as Mary did, that God is with us. God will be with us during good surprises and challenging surprises.
- **Pray:** God of Peace, thank you for sending the gift of your son. As we prepare to celebrate his birth, help us remember that nothing is impossible for you, and you are always with us. Amen.

Angel Ornament Patterns

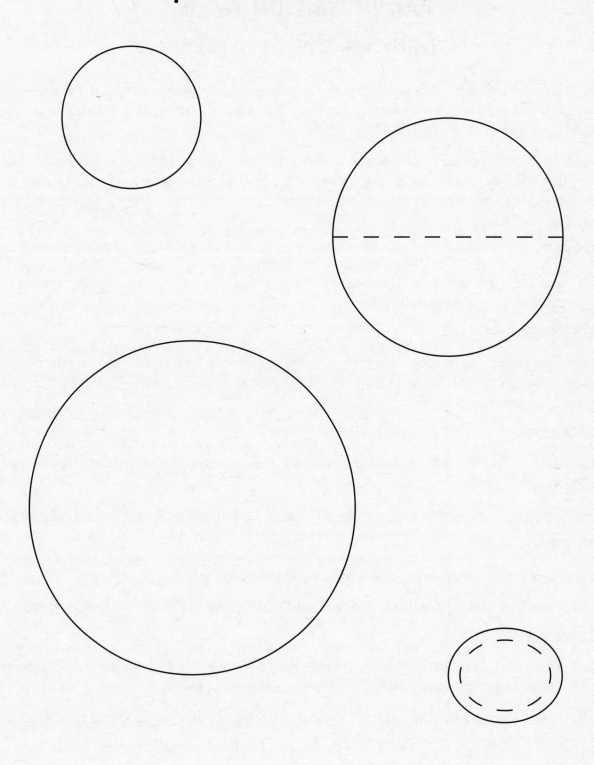

Surprised by God: Gabriel Visits Mary

Do you like surprises? This is a story about surprises. It's a story from the Bible about a woman named Mary. You've probably heard about her. She was the mother of Jesus. (I know you've heard of him!)

When Mary was a young girl, about twelve or thirteen years old, she was engaged to Joseph. Girls got married at a much younger age back then. Mary was still living in her father's house, since she and Joseph weren't married yet. One day God sent an angel to visit Mary.

SURPRISE!

That was the first surprise. The angel's name was Gabriel. He told Mary, "Rejoice, favored one! The Lord is with you!"

SURPRISE!

Mary was surprised and confused by the angel's words. She didn't know what they meant. The angel said, "Don't be afraid, Mary. God is honoring you. You are pregnant and will give birth to a son."

SURPRISE!

Mary said, "You must be mistaken, because I'm engaged to Joseph but we're not married yet."

"No, I'm right," said Gabriel. "The baby will be God's son, and you will name him Jesus."

SURPRISE!

Can you imagine Mary's surprise when she learned she was going to have God's son?

"I have another message for you," Gabriel said. "Your cousin Elizabeth is pregnant too."

SURPRISE!

That news was a surprise because Elizabeth was very old and didn't have any children yet. Gabriel said, "Remember that nothing is impossible for God."

"That's not a surprise," said Mary. "I know God will be with me, and if this is what God wants me to do, then I will do it."

Based on Luke 1:26-38

3 Chosen by God

Objectives

The children will
- hear Luke 1:39-55.
- discover that Mary visited her cousin, Elizabeth, after she learned they were both pregnant.
- learn that Mary praised God for choosing her.
- explore the idea of being claimed by God in their lives.

Theme

God chose Mary to give birth to Jesus.

Bible Verse

I have called you by name; you are mine. (Isaiah 43:1b)

Focus for the Teacher

The Gospel of Luke begins with the announcements of two upcoming births. The first announcement was to Elizabeth and Zechariah. Zechariah and Elizabeth had no children, and they were getting old. It is likely they had accepted that they would remain childless. Enter an angel sent from God who surprised them with the news that not only would they have a son but also their son would have an important job to do for God. Their son would prepare people for the coming of the Lord (Luke 1:17).

The second birth announcement in Luke is the story of Gabriel telling Mary that she would give birth to God's son. Gabriel also told Mary that her cousin Elizabeth was expecting a baby. The two separate story lines merged when Mary went to visit Elizabeth.

When Elizabeth heard Mary's greeting, her child leaped in her womb. Elizabeth told Mary that the baby jumped for joy in the presence of the Lord, even though there is no indication that Elizabeth knew of Mary's pregnancy prior to the visit. When her baby jumped for joy, Elizabeth took this as a sign. Elizabeth's baby, who grew up to become

> Joy is a recurring theme in the Gospel of Luke.

John the Baptist, identified Jesus as Lord even when they were both still in the womb.

Upon seeing Mary, Elizabeth was filled with the Holy Spirit and made several pronouncements. She said that God had blessed Mary and the child she carried. Elizabeth also noted that Mary had been given the honor of the Lord visiting her. Even though an angel had told Mary she was pregnant with God's son, it must have been reassuring for Mary to receive this affirmation from Elizabeth.

Elizabeth's baby jumped for joy. Mary responded to Elizabeth's greeting with a joyful song of praise. Joy is a recurring theme in the Gospel of Luke. As mentioned, the Gospel begins with the joyous announcements of two pregnancies. There are the joyous proclamations of what the future holds for the children of these two women. Throughout Jesus' ministry there is the joy of forgiveness, healings, raising the dead, and receiving the outcasts. The Gospel ends with the joy of the disciples following their realization that Jesus is alive. As you continue to celebrate Advent with your children, experience the joy of this season.

34

Explore Interest Groups

Be sure that adult leaders are waiting when the first child arrives. Greet and welcome the children. Get the children involved in an activity that interests them and introduces the theme for the day's activities.

Make a Shiny Ornament

- Show the children the wrapped box.

- **Ask:** Do you remember who gave the first Christmas present? (God) And what was the present? (Jesus)

- Have the children help you open the wrapped box.

- **Say:** Today we are making two more Christmas ornaments. As with the last two weeks, one of the ornaments will be for you to keep, and one of them will be for you to give to someone else. When your ornaments are made, you may use the supplies in this box to wrap one of them.

- Give each child four pieces of cardboard and four pieces of aluminum foil.

- Have each child wrap a piece of aluminum foil around each of their pieces of cardboard. Show them how to lay the foil on top of the cardboard, smooth it flat, and wrap the excess foil around to the back of the cardboard.

- Have each child use a piece of tape to secure the foil on the back.

- Have each child cut a piece of ribbon 6 to 8 inches long, fold it in half, and tape both ends of the ribbon to the back of one of the foil-wrapped cardboard pieces. The ribbon should extend beyond the edge of the cardboard to form a hanging loop. Have each child cut another piece of ribbon and tape it to one of the other cardboard squares in the same way.

- Have each child lay their cardboard pieces in front of them with the smooth foil-wrapped side up.

- Let each child use the blunt end of a pen, an unsharpened pencil, or a wooden craft stick to write the word *Joy* in the foil. Tell them to press gently so the foil does not tear.

- Encourage the children to experiment with different etching techniques and to add designs to their ornaments.

- When the designs are finished, have each child put glue on the backs of the foil-wrapped squares with the ribbons and glue each square to one of the other squares, back to back, to complete their two ornaments.

- Have the children wrap one of their ornaments and decide whom they will give it to.

Prepare

✓ Provide corrugated cardboard, aluminum foil, ribbon, scissors, tape, and glue.

✓ Provide pens, unsharpened pencils, or wooden craft sticks as etching tools.

✓ Cut the cardboard into 3-inch squares. You will need four squares of cardboard for each child.

✓ Tear pieces of aluminum foil approximately 4 inches square. The exact size of the foil is not important, as long as it is big enough to cover one side of the cardboard square.

✓ Use the wrapped box prepared for Lesson 1 filled with gift-wrapping supplies. You may choose to add new wrapping paper to the box.

Prepare

✓ Provide white paper, crayons, watercolor paints, paintbrushes, plastic containers for water, and plastic table coverings or newspaper.

✓ Protect the work area with plastic table coverings or newspaper.

✓ Fill plastic containers one-third full with water and place them in the center of the table with the watercolor paints.

Prepare

✓ Form a circle of chairs facing inward, using one less chair than the number of children playing the game.

Called by Name Art

- **Say:** Your name is special. It's one of the ways people identify you. Our Bible verse for today tells us that God calls each one of us by name and chooses us to be a child of God.

- Have each child use a crayon to write his or her name on a piece of paper. Encourage children to use big letters or block letters to cover most of the page.

- Show the children how to use the watercolor paints by dipping a paintbrush in water, mixing it with the paint, and then painting on the paper.

- Encourage each child to paint a design over their name, covering the entire page and noticing that the crayon shows through the paint.

Child of God Scramble

- Choose one child to stand in the center of the circle of chairs. Have the rest of the children sit in the chairs.

- Explain the following rules to the children:
    o Clap . . . your elbows together.
    o The person in the center will say, "I am a child of God that . . ." and complete the statement by saying something that is true about him or her. For example: "I am a child of God that is nine years old," "I am a child of God that has short hair," or "I am a child of God that likes to play chess."
    o Every person in the circle for whom that statement is true must get up and find a new seat at least two chairs away from where they were sitting, while the person in the middle tries to get a seat also.
    o The person left standing becomes the next person to stand in the middle.

- Encourage the children to play the game.

Large Group

Bring all the children together to experience the Bible story. Use a bell to alert the children to the large-group time.

Praise God

- **Say:** In today's Bible story we will hear about Mary praising God for choosing her to be the mother of God's son. It's good to praise God for choosing us. God chooses us to be children of God. Let's praise God right now for that. I will call out an action such as "Clap!" We will then do that action seven times and then say, "Praise God!"

- Give the following directions and encourage the children to do each action seven times and then say, "Praise God!"
    - o Clap
    - o Snap
    - o Stomp
    - o Nod
    - o Jump

Chosen by God: Mary Praises God

- **Say:** Last week we heard about the angel Gabriel visiting Mary.

- **Ask:** What did Gabriel tell Mary? (That she was pregnant with God's son. That her cousin Elizabeth was also pregnant.)

- **Say:** Today's Bible story tells what happened after Gabriel's visit.

- Read the Bible story from "Chosen by God: Mary Praises God."

- **Say:** After Gabriel's visit, Mary must have been wondering if Gabriel's message was true. It was probably reassuring to hear Elizabeth tell her that God had chosen Mary to carry this special baby.

- **Ask:** What was Mary's response to Elizabeth's greeting? (She sang a song of praise to God.)

Prepare

✓ Provide a copy for each child of **Reproducible 3a: Chosen by God: Mary Praises God**, found at the end of this lesson.

Jumping Joyful Bible Verse

- Show the children the Bible verse. Encourage them to read the verse together with you.

- **Say:** This verse is a message from God for us. It is a joyful thing that God has chosen us as God's people. Each of us is a child of God. We are going to say the verse again, but this time we are going to jump for joy as we say each word.

- Encourage the children to say the verse while jumping.

- Repeat the verse several times.

Prepare

✓ Write the Bible verse on a marker board or a piece of mural paper and place it where it can easily be seen. (I have called you by name; you are mine. Isaiah 43:1b)

Prepare

✓ Provide tape to attach the word to the outside of the box.

Joyfully Chosen

- **Say:** So far we have opened two of the purple presents in our special Advent wreath.

- **Ask:** What words have we found so far? (*Hope* and *Peace*)

- **Say:** Today we will open the pink present.

- Invite a child to open the pink present containing the word *Joy* and show the class what is inside. Tape the word *Joy* to the outside of the present.

- **Say:** Today we unwrap and receive the gift of joy.

- Lead the children in the following cheer:

    Leader: Give me an J!
    Children: J!

    Leader: Give me an O!
    Children: O!

    Leader: Give me a Y!
    Children: Y!

    Leader: What's that spell?
    Children: Joy!

    Leader: One more time!
    Children: Joy!

- **Say:** The word *Joy* reminds us that Elizabeth's baby jumped for joy when Elizabeth saw Mary. Mary could have responded to the news that she was carrying God's son in many ways. She chose to respond with a joyful song of praise.

- **Say:** Today we are going to learn another breath prayer. As we pray, we will take slow breaths in and out. As we breathe in, I will say, "God of Joy," and as we breathe out, I will say, "We praise you." I will say the prayer three times.

- Have the children breathe in and out slowly while you pray.

- **Say:** During the next week, remember to be joyful. Take some time to say this breath prayer to yourself.

- Dismiss children to their small groups.

Small Groups

Divide the children into small groups. You may organize the groups around age levels or around readers and nonreaders. Keep the groups small, with a maximum of ten children in each group. You may need to have more than one group of each age level.

Young Children (Ages 5–7)

- **Say:** Mary praised God for choosing her. It's a good thing to praise and thank God for choosing us and for being with us always.

- Show the children the mural paper.

- Invite the children to use markers to write sentences of praise all over the paper. Examples of praise sentences: I love you, God! Thank you, God! I praise you all the time, God!

- **Ask:** What did Elizabeth's baby do when Mary greeted Elizabeth? (Jump for joy)

- **Say:** Sometimes when we are happy and joyful, it's hard to stay still. When we are joyful, we want to celebrate and share that joy with other people.

- **Ask:** What makes you feel joyful? Has there ever been a time when you wanted to jump for joy?

- Allow the children an opportunity to share.

- Have the children stand up.

- **Say:** We are going to end our time together by jumping for joy. I will say a name, and that person will jump in the air and say, "Joy!" When that person lands, he or she will say someone else's name. That person will then jump in the air and say, "Joy!" naming someone else when he or she lands.

- Have the children take turns jumping for joy.

- **Pray:** God of Joy, we thank you for Jesus. Help us to share the joy of your love with other people. Amen.

Prepare

- Provide mural paper and markers.

- Cut a large sheet of mural paper, and use a marker to write the words "Praise God" in the center of the paper.

Prepare

✓ Provide pencils and a copy for each child of **Reproducible 3b: Write a Poem of Praise**, found at the end of this lesson.

Older Children (Ages 8–11)

- **Say:** Mary praised God for choosing her. It's a good thing to praise and thank God for choosing us and for being present with us always.

- Give each child a pencil and a copy of "Write a Poem of Praise."

- Invite each child to follow the instructions to write a poem. Offer encouragement and assistance as necessary.

- Encourage the children to share their poems with one another.

- **Say:** We're going to end our time together by praising God while we play a rhythm game. The rhythm we will do is tapping our knees with our hands two times, clapping two times, and then snapping our fingers two times, once with each hand. Let's try it.

- Lead the children in doing the rhythm a couple of times.

- **Say:** Now we will add words. As we tap, one person will say, "Praise God." As we clap, that person will say, "Right now." And as we snap, that person will say someone's name. The next time we do the rhythm, the person who has been named will say, "Praise God right now," as above, and name someone else. Let's see how long we can keep our rhythm going.

- Choose a person to start and play the game.

- **Say:** We are getting closer to celebrating Christmas. That's another reason to joyfully praise God.

- **Pray:** God of Joy, thank you for choosing us. We are thankful to be your children and give our praise only to you. Amen.

Under Wraps: Children's Leader Guide

Chosen by God:
Mary Praises God

When the angel Gabriel told Mary she was going to have a baby, he told her that her cousin Elizabeth was also pregnant. Although her cousin Elizabeth was very old, she didn't have any children. Mary was amazed that Elizabeth would be having a baby now in her old age.

Mary went to visit Elizabeth. When Elizabeth heard Mary's greeting, her baby leaped inside of her and Elizabeth was filled with the Holy Spirit. As soon as Elizabeth saw Mary, she knew that God had blessed Mary with a very special child. She told Mary, "God has blessed you and chosen you to carry a special child. When I heard your voice, my baby jumped for joy!"

Elizabeth's baby grew up to be John the Baptist, who prepared the way for Jesus. Even before he was born, John was letting people know that Jesus was special.

The angel Gabriel told Mary that her baby was God's son. Elizabeth confirmed that Mary's baby was special. In response to Elizabeth's greeting, Mary sang a song of praise to God for choosing her.

"With all my heart I praise God!
I am filled with joy.
God has chosen me
and blessed me.
God's name is holy.
God shows mercy to everyone.
God made a covenant with Abraham
and his descendants.
God has done many great things.
I praise God for all God has done
and for all God will do in the future.
God's name is holy!"

Based on Luke 1:39-55

Write a Poem of Praise

God chose Mary to be the mother of God's son. God has also chosen us to be children of God. That is joyful news and definitely reason for praise! Use the instructions and template below to write a poem praising God. Remember that poems don't have to rhyme.

Write a "praise sentence" that tells of your love for God. For example, "Praise God who is all around me!" or "I will love you forever, God!"

Write a sentence describing how it feels to know that God has chosen you and called you by name.

Write your praise sentence again.

Think about a time you have known that God was with you. Write a sentence about that experience.

Write your praise sentence again.

4 Loved by God

Objectives

The children will
- hear Luke 2:1-7.
- discover that Jesus was born in Bethlehem.
- learn that Jesus' birth was a gift from God given out of God's love.
- explore the idea of being loved by God in their lives.

Theme

Jesus was God's gift of love to the world.

Bible Verse

God so loved the world that he gave his only Son, so that everyone who believes in him won't perish but will have eternal life. (John 3:16)

Focus for the Teacher

Each year during the Christmas season, we journey to Bethlehem—not literally, of course, as few of us could afford the time or expense to travel there once a year. However, in order to meaningfully celebrate Christmas, we place ourselves in the story each year, reading the familiar words that lead us to Bethlehem.

Jesus' birth took place in Bethlehem—a small town that was relatively unimportant at the time. God's son was born to a young couple from Nazareth. Since Joseph and Mary were from Nazareth, how did it come to be that Jesus was born in Bethlehem? In Luke 2:1-5, we discover that Joseph and Mary journeyed to Bethlehem in response to a decree from Caesar Augustus. Joseph and Mary were going about the business of their life and complying with Roman law. While they were in Bethlehem, Jesus was born. Some of us journey to Bethlehem as Joseph and Mary did, in the midst of going about the business of our lives. No matter what that business may be, how seemingly important or seemingly insignificant, God's son comes into the midst of it every year and draws us to Bethlehem to celebrate his birth.

> God's son was born to a young couple from Nazareth.

Although our lesson this week focuses on Joseph and Mary, they weren't the only ones who journeyed to Bethlehem. The shepherds came to Bethlehem too. They came as the result of a heavenly declaration. The angels told the shepherds of the marvelous thing that had occurred in Bethlehem, and off the shepherds went to see for themselves. Some people experience the Christmas story in this way, coming to Bethlehem as the result of a dramatic spiritual experience.

And then there were the magi, wise men who were scholars and studied and interpreted the movements of stars and planets. Their learning led them to Bethlehem. There are people today who journey to Bethlehem through scholarly activities and study, just as the wise men did.

There are many routes that one may take, but they all lead to Bethlehem. As we reenter the story, we are reminded that many years ago in this small, ordinary town, God loved the world so much that God did something extraordinary. A baby was born, God's son, who would be a peaceful ruler and change the world forever. What a gift of love!

Explore Interest Groups

Be sure that adult leaders are waiting when the first child arrives. Greet and welcome the children. Get the children involved in an activity that interests them and introduces the theme for the day's activities.

Make Candy Cane Heart Ornaments

- Show the children the wrapped box.

- **Ask:** What do you think we will find in our box today?

- Have the children help you open the wrapped box.

- **Say:** All month we have been making ornaments that remind us of the story of Jesus' birth. Today you will make ornaments that are reminders of God's love for us. You will make two ornaments, one to keep and one to give to someone else. When your ornaments are made, you may use the wrapping supplies to wrap one of them.

- Give each child two candy canes.

- Show the children how to lay two candy canes in front of them so they form a heart.

- **Say:** We will make our ornaments in the shape of a heart to remind us that God loves us and that's why God sent Jesus.

- Have each child cut three pieces of yarn, each approximately 8 inches long.

- Have each child tie a piece of yarn at the top of the heart where the two candy canes meet, securing the candy canes together by tying a knot. Have each child tie the ends of the same piece of yarn together to form a hanging loop.

- Have the children tie one piece of yarn around the bottom of each candy cane. Have them tie a knot and then cut off one of the yarn tails close to the knot, leaving the other yarn tail attached.

- Have the children take the two yarn tails and tie them together, pulling the yarn tight so that the candy canes form a heart shape. Instruct the children to tie a knot to hold the candy canes together and then tie a bow with the remaining yarn tails.

- If desired, have the children tie ribbon onto their candy cane hearts for extra decoration.

- Give each child two more candy canes to make a second ornament.

- Have children wrap one of their ornaments and decide whom they will give it to.

- **Say:** When you give your second ornament to someone, remind them that God loves them.

Prepare

✓ Provide large individually wrapped candy canes (four per child), along with scissors, yarn, and ribbon.

✓ Use the wrapped box prepared for Lesson 1 filled with gift-wrapping supplies. You may choose to add new wrapping paper to the box.

Prepare

✓ Decide where you will play this game. It can be played in the classroom, or it can be played as you are traveling from your room to another place.

A Journey Game

- Have the children line up from youngest to oldest.

- **Say:** Pretend that you are going on a trip and you can only take one thing. What would you take with you?

- Give the children a minute to decide on something to take.

- **Say:** We are going to play a journey game. The person at the front of the line will be the leader and lead us for about five steps. Then the leader will stop and say, "I'm going on a journey, and I'm taking a _____."

- Instruct the child to fill in the blank with the object they have chosen.

- **Say:** The leader will then go to the back of the line. The next person will lead the group for five steps, and then they will stop and say, "I'm going on a journey, and I'm taking a (object named by first child) and a _____."

- Explain that the game will continue in this way until every child has had a chance·to be the leader and the list is long.

- If you are leaving the room on your journey, tell the children where you are headed so the leaders know where to go.

- When all children have had a chance to add to the list, ask for volunteers to try to recite the entire list.

Prepare

✓ Provide white paper, construction paper, scissors, glue, crayons, markers, and colored pencils.

✓ Obtain a variety of picture books about Jesus' birth. A trip to the public library should be helpful if your church does not have a children's library. Try to find books with a variety of art styles.

Visualize the Christmas Story

- Have the children spend time looking at the picture books.

- Encourage them to notice the similarities and differences in the pictures that all depict the same story.

- Invite each child to use the art materials provided to make their own picture of the Christmas story.

Large Group

Bring all the children together to experience the Bible story. Use a bell to alert the children to the large-group time.

Infinite Love

- **Ask:** What does *infinity* mean? (Never-ending, going on forever)

- **Say:** God's love for us is infinite. It will never end. The symbol for infinity looks like the number 8 lying on its side.

- Have the children stand up.

- Encourage each child to make an infinity symbol in the air with the index finger of one hand and continue making the symbol over and over.

- Encourage each child to try making an infinity symbol with the index finger of the other hand at the same time.

- Have the children try making the two infinity symbols going in opposite directions at the same time and going in the same direction at the same time.

Loved by God: Jesus Is Born!

- **Say:** It is almost Christmas! Our story today is about Jesus' birth. This is what we will celebrate when Christmas comes this week.

- Read the story from "Loved by God: Jesus Is Born!" as you walk around the room. At each stop you make, read a different section of the story, and share and discuss the related information below that section of the story.

- **Say:** Jesus was the gift that God gave to the world on that first Christmas Day. God sent Jesus to show us a better way to live and to teach us what God wants us to do.

Prepare

- ✓ Provide for each child a copy of **Reproducible 4a: Loved by God: Jesus Is Born!** found at the end of this lesson.

- ✓ Plan a route around the room, and decide on five places you can stand as you tell today's story.

Loud Soft Bible Verse

- Show the children the Bible verse.

- Encourage the children to read the verse together with you.

- **Say:** We are going to read the verse again, but this time we are going to alternate saying the words loudly and softly. We will say the first word loud, the second word soft, the third word loud, and so forth.

- Encourage the children to read the verse together with you as directed.

- **Ask:** Why did God send Jesus into the world? (Because God loves us.)

Prepare

- ✓ Write the Bible verse on a marker board or a piece of mural paper, and place it where it can easily be seen. (God so loved the world that he gave his only Son, so that everyone who believes in him won't perish but will have eternal life. John 3:16)

Prepare

✓ Provide tape to attach the word to the outside of the box.

Loved

- **Say:** So far we have opened three of the presents in our special Advent wreath.

- **Ask:** What words have we found so far? (*Hope, Peace, Joy*)

- **Say:** Today we will open the last purple present.

- Invite a child to open the purple present containing the word *Love* and show the class what is inside. Tape the word *Love* to the outside of the present.

- **Say:** Today we unwrap and receive the gift of love.

- Lead the children in the following cheer:
  Leader: Give me an L!
  Children: L!
  Leader: Give me an O!
  Children: O!
  Leader: Give me a V!
  Children: V!
  Leader: Give me an E!
  Children: E!
  Leader: What's that spell?
  Children: Love!
  Leader: One more time!
  Children: Love!

- **Say:** The word *Love* reminds us that God loves us more than we can imagine. God sent Jesus into the world as a gift of love.

- **Say:** Today we are going to learn another breath prayer. As we pray, we will take slow breaths in and out. As we breathe in, I will say, "God of Love," and as we breathe out, I will say, "Thank you for Jesus." I will say the prayer three times.

- Have the children breathe in and out slowly while you pray.

- **Say:** During the next week as Christmas gets closer, remember to thank God for Jesus. Take some time to say this breath prayer to yourself.

- Dismiss children to their small groups.

Under Wraps: Children's Leader Guide

Small Groups

Divide the children into small groups. You may organize the groups around age levels or around readers and nonreaders. Keep the groups small, with a maximum of ten children in each group. You may need to have more than one group of each age level.

Young Children (Ages 5–7)

- **Say:** It's almost Christmas! Today we heard the story of Jesus' birth. I'm going to invite you to close your eyes as I read the story to you again. As you listen to the story with your eyes closed, imagine that you are in the story. Imagine what you might have seen and heard if you had been there.

- Invite the children to close their eyes.

- Read Luke 2:1-7 from a CEB translation of the Bible.

- Invite the children to open their eyes.

- **Ask:** What did you imagine seeing? What sounds might you have heard?

- Give children an opportunity to share.

- **Say:** God loves each of you and will never stop loving you. It's because of God's amazing love that Jesus was born.

- Give each child a copy of "Letter from God."

- **Say:** Here is a letter for you to take home to remind you how much God loves you.

- Invite each child to write his or her name on the letter.

- Encourage each child to decorate the letter.

- **Say:** As you celebrate Jesus' birth, remember how much God loves you.

- **Pray:** God of Love, as we remember and celebrate the birth of your son, help us remember your extraordinary love. Thank you for loving us so much. Help us to share your love with others. Amen.

Prepare

- Provide each child with crayons and a copy of **Reproducible 4b: Letter from God**, found at the end of this lesson.

Prepare

✓ Cut a big piece of mural paper and use a marker to divide it into three columns.

✓ At the top of the first column write "Ordinary" and at the top of the third column write "Extraordinary." Across the middle column write "Plus God's Love" in big letters.

✓ Lay the paper on a table or on the floor where the children will be able to see it.

Older Children (Ages 8–11)

• Have the children sit where they can see the mural paper.

• **Ask:** Who can tell me what the word *ordinary* means? (Regular, common) What does *extraordinary* mean? (Exceptional, beyond what is expected)

• On the mural paper, write "Bethlehem" in the ordinary column.

• **Say:** Before Jesus' birth, Bethlehem was an ordinary town. It wasn't very big and was probably considered unimportant by most people. But God used Bethlehem for a special purpose.

• **Ask:** How did God make Bethlehem extraordinary? (God chose Bethlehem to be the birthplace of Jesus.)

• On the mural paper, write "Birthplace of Jesus" in the extraordinary column.

• **Say:** God has a wonderful way of taking places, things, and people that might be considered ordinary and making them extraordinary. Let's look at some other examples from the story of Jesus' birth.

• List the following words one at a time in the ordinary column, and discuss with the children how God made the person, place, or thing extraordinary.

• Mary (Young girl who had never been married became the mother of Jesus, God's son)

• Elizabeth (Old woman who became John the Baptist's mother)

• Joseph (Carpenter who became Jesus' earthly father)

• Manger (Feeding trough for animals that became a crib for Jesus)

• Write the word "You" in the ordinary column.

• **Say:** Some people might say that each of you is an ordinary child. But we know that God uses ordinary things and makes them extraordinary. Maybe you are extraordinary because you are really good at showing others God's love by sharing hugs or maybe God has given you a special talent. Spend a few moments thinking in silence about how God makes you extraordinary.

• Give the children a few moments to think about this, and then write "In Many Ways" in the extraordinary column.

• **Say:** Each of you is extraordinary in your own way because God loves you. It is because of God's extraordinary love that Jesus was born. As you celebrate Jesus' birth, remember how much God loves you.

• **Pray:** God of Love, as we remember and celebrate the birth of your son, help us remember your extraordinary love. Thank you for loving us so much. Help us to share your love with others. Amen.

Loved by God: Jesus Is Born!

1. In those days Caesar Augustus declared that everyone throughout the empire should be enrolled in the tax lists.

 Do we live in an empire?
 Caesar Augustus was the emperor. Do we have an emperor?

2. In those days Caesar Augustus declared that everyone throughout the empire should be enrolled in the tax lists. This first enrollment occurred when Quirinius governed Syria.

 An enrollment was a type of census. It was used to keep track of people for taxation.
 Who is the governor of our state?

3. In those days Caesar Augustus declared that everyone throughout the empire should be enrolled in the tax lists. This first enrollment occurred when Quirinius governed Syria. Everyone went to their own cities to be enrolled.

 Going to "your own city" means traveling to the place your ancestors were born.
 Where would you have to go if you had to travel to your birthplace to be registered?

4. In those days Caesar Augustus declared that everyone throughout the empire should be enrolled in the tax lists. This first enrollment occurred when Quirinius governed Syria. Everyone went to their own cities to be enrolled. Since Joseph belonged to David's house and family line, he went up from the city of Nazareth in Galilee to David's city, called Bethlehem, in Judea.

 Why did Joseph travel to Bethlehem?
 Where was he traveling from?
 How did Joseph travel? By car? On donkey?

5. In those days Caesar Augustus declared that everyone throughout the empire should be enrolled in the tax lists. This first enrollment occurred when Quirinius governed Syria. Everyone went to their own cities to be enrolled. Since Joseph belonged to David's house and family line, he went up from the city of Nazareth in Galilee to David's city, called Bethlehem, in Judea. He went to be enrolled together with Mary, who was promised to him in marriage and who was pregnant. While they were there, the time came for Mary to have her baby. She gave birth to her firstborn child, a son, wrapped him snugly, and laid him in a manger, because there was no place for them in the guestroom.

 Who in the story was born in Bethlehem?
 A manger is a feeding trough for animals. Why did Mary lay Jesus in a manger?

Based on Luke 2:1-7

Letter from God

Dear

I love you so much!
I will never stop loving you!

Love,
God

A Season of Joy

Objectives

The children will
- hear Luke 2:8-20.
- discover that shepherds visited Jesus following his birth.
- learn that Jesus' birth resulted in great joy.
- explore reactions of joy in their lives.

Theme

Celebrating Jesus' birth is a reason for joy.

Bible Verse

The shepherds returned home, glorifying and praising God for all they had heard and seen.
Luke 2:20a

Focus for the Teacher

Although we hear the story every year, the message of the Christmas story remains inspiring and empowering. God did not choose to make a flashy and attention-getting entrance. Instead God chose to reveal God's presence with us through the birth of a baby born in humble circumstances.

It is doubtful that the shepherds, as they began another evening of watching over their sheep, expected a visit from an angel. At the time of Jesus, shepherds were considered by some people to be second-class citizens. Yet an angel did visit them! As surprising as the visit from an angel was, the purpose of the visit must have been just as surprising. The angel announced that a Savior had been born in Bethlehem. It had been 700 years since Isaiah foretold the birth of a Messiah. Could it really be happening now? And a manger was probably not where people expected to find their Savior.

In response to this surprising angelic announcement, the shepherds hurried off

> The angel announced that a Savior had been born in Bethlehem.

to Bethlehem. We've heard the shepherds' story so many times that it may seem natural to us that they responded in this way. But wasn't the shepherds' response almost as surprising as the angel's visit? They didn't wait a couple of weeks until they could arrange for someone to watch their sheep so they could take a vacation. They didn't say, "That's interesting, and next time we're in Bethlehem we'll check it out." No, Luke tells us that the shepherds went "quickly" to find Mary and Joseph and the child of whom they had been told.

This story that we hear every year reminds us that God works in unexpected ways and appears in unexpected places. God chose to reveal God's presence in a surprising way. We too may experience God's presence in unexpected and surprising places in our own lives. Regardless of how or where we experience God's presence, there is only one possible response to make. With the shepherds, we respond with joy and share the good news of God's love.

Explore Interest Groups

Be sure that adult leaders are waiting when the first child arrives. Greet and welcome the children. Get the children involved in an activity that interests them and introduces the theme for the day's activities.

Paint a Picture of Joy

- **Say:** All month we have been preparing and waiting for Christmas. Now Christmas is here! Christmas is a time of joy as we celebrate God's great gift of Jesus.

- Invite each child to draw a joyful picture, using crayons or markers.

Prepare

✓ Provide paper and crayons or markers.

Who's the Shepherd?

- **Say:** The shepherds were the first ones to hear about the birth of Jesus. They heard the good news from an angel. Being a shepherd in Jesus' day was difficult work. Shepherds spent most of their time outside watching their flocks. They had to move the sheep around in search of food. We are going to play a game today called "Who's the Shepherd?"

- **Say:** Here is how the game is played. One child will be the angel. The angel will go where he or she cannot see or hear what the rest of us are doing. The rest of us will choose one person to be the shepherd. The rest of us will be sheep. Then we will all walk or stand around the area pretending we are in a field. The shepherd is the leader. Every once in awhile the shepherd will say, "Baa," and the rest of us will follow by saying, "Baa." The angel will return and try to determine by listening closely who the shepherd is. The angel will go to the shepherd and say, "Good news! Jesus is born!" If the angel has guessed correctly, the shepherd will say, "I'm going to Bethlehem!" If the shepherd delivers the message to a sheep, the sheep will say, "Baa." The angel will get three tries to correctly guess the identity of the shepherd.

- Play the game with the children.

- Choose a new angel and shepherd and continue playing.

Jesus Was His Name Oh!

- Teach the children the words to the following song sung to the tune of "B-I-N-G-O."

    God sent his son into the world, and Jesus was his name oh!
    J-E-S-U-S
    J-E-S-U-S
    J-E-S-U-S
    And Jesus was his name oh!

- Once the children have learned the song, lead them in singing the song through six times in the following manner:
    1. Sing all words
    2. Substitute claps for each "J"
    3. Substitute two claps for each "J-E"
    4. Substitute three claps for each "J-E-S"
    5. Substitute four claps for each "J-E-S-U"
    6. Substitute five claps for each "J-E-S-U-S"

Prepare

✓ Provide unfrosted cupcakes, frosting, wooden craft sticks, colored sugar or sprinkles for decoration, paper plates, and "Happy Birthday" napkins.

Birthday Party for Jesus

- Have the children wash their hands.

- **Say:** Today we are going to have a birthday party for Jesus.

- Give each child a napkin.

- Give each child a cupcake on a paper plate and a wooden craft stick with some frosting on it.

- Encourage each child to frost his or her cupcake and decorate it.

- When all the cupcakes are decorated, join in singing "Happy Birthday" to Jesus.

- Say a prayer thanking God for Jesus.

- Enjoy your snack together.

Large Group

Bring all the children together to experience the Bible story. Use a bell to alert the children to the large-group time.

Sound It Out

- **Say:** Imagine you were in a field with a bunch of shepherds and a bunch of sheep.

- **Ask:** What do you think it would sound like?

- Encourage the children to make sounds they might hear.

- **Say:** Imagine that you suddenly saw a bright light and an angel in the sky. Show me what it would sound like if all the shepherds and all the sheep were suddenly quiet.

- Have the children go to the large-group area and sit down.

Loved by God: Jesus Is Born!

- **Say:** Last time we met, we heard the story of Jesus' birth. Today we will hear about something that happened after Jesus was born.

- Read the Bible story from "A Season of Joy."

- **Ask:** Who were the first ones to hear about Jesus' birth? (The shepherds) How did they hear the news? (An angel told them.) What did they do when they heard the news? (They went immediately to Bethlehem.)

- **Say:** Remember that the prophet Isaiah had foretold the birth of Jesus, but that was 700 years before Jesus was born. People had been waiting for Jesus to be born for more than 700 years. No wonder the shepherds were excited when they heard the news!

Prepare

✓ Provide a copy for each child of **Reproducible 5a: A Season of Joy**, found at the end of this lesson.

Prepare

✓ Write the Bible verse on a marker board or a piece of mural paper, and place it where it can easily be seen. (The shepherds returned home, glorifying and praising God for all they had heard and seen. Luke 2:20a)

Prepare

✓ Provide tape to attach the word to the outside of the box.

Spreading Bible Verse

- Show the children the Bible verse.

- Encourage the children to read the Bible verse with you.

- Choose a child in the middle of the room to begin the Bible verse.

- **Say:** (Child's name) is going to read the Bible verse. Then they will say the verse again and anyone sitting next to them or directly in front of them or directly behind them will join in and read the verse too. We will keep repeating the verse over and over. When the person next to you or in front of you or behind you says the verse, then the next time you will join in with us.

- Begin saying the verse and continue repeating it until everyone is saying the verse together.

Loved

- **Say:** So far we have opened four of the presents in our special Advent wreath. The only present we have left to open is the white present in the middle of our wreath.

- **Ask:** What words have we found so far? (*Hope, Peace, Joy, Love*)

- Invite a child to open the white present containing the word Jesus and show the class what is inside. Tape the word *Jesus* to the outside of the present.

- **Say:** Today we unwrap and receive the greatest gift of all, Jesus.

- Lead the children in the following cheer:
  Leader: Give me an J!
  Children: J!
  Leader: Give me an E!
  Children: E!
  Leader: Give me a S!
  Children: S!
  Leader: Give me an U!
  Children: U!
  Leader: Give me an S!
  Children: S!
  Leader: What's that spell?
  Children: Jesus!
  Leader: Whose birthday do we celebrate at Christmas
  Children: Love!

- **Say:** God sent Jesus into the world as a gift of love. That is good news and a reason to be joyful.

- Dismiss children to their small groups.

Small Groups

Divide the children into small groups. You may organize the groups around age levels or around readers and nonreaders. Keep the groups small, with a maximum of ten children in each group. You may need to have more than one group of each age level.

Young Children (Ages 5–7)

- Give each child a copy of Life as a Shepherd in Bible Times.

- Read through the information together as a group.

- **Ask:** Based on this information, do you think some people were surprised that shepherds were the first ones to hear about Jesus' birth? Why?

- **Say:** Although some people looked down on shepherds, God did not. God's gift of Jesus is for everyone.

- Invite each child to choose a person who is part of the Christmas story.

- Encourage each child to think about the person they have chosen and imagine the words they might have said at the time of Jesus' birth. For example, Mary might say, "I never thought I would have to use a manger for my baby's bed."

- Encourage the children to take turns acting like the person they have chosen without telling the person's name.

- Invite the other children to guess the person being acted out.

- **Pray:** God, thank you for your son, Jesus. We remember his birth and celebrate with joy. Help us to remember the joy we feel all year long. Amen.

Prepare

- Provide for each child a copy of **Reproducible 5b: Life as a Shepherd in Bible Times**, found at the end of this lesson.

Prepare

✓ Provide each child with a copy of **Reproducible 5b: Life as a Shepherd in Bible Times**, found at the end of this lesson.

✓ Provide a beanbag.

✓ Note: If you do not have a beanbag, use a clean sock rolled into a ball.

Older Children (Ages 8–11)

- Give each child a copy of "Life as a Shepherd in Bible Times."

- Allow the children time to read the information silently.

- **Ask:** Based on this information, do you think some people were surprised that shepherds were the first ones to hear about Jesus' birth? Why?

- **Say:** Although some people looked down on shepherds, God did not. God's gift of Jesus is for everyone.

- Ask: What are the four words that we discovered in our Advent wreath boxes? (*Hope, Joy, Peace, Love*)

- **Say:** I am going to toss the beanbag to one of you and say one of those four words--*Hope, Joy, Peace,* or *Love*. When you catch the beanbag, tell us something about the Christmas story that relates to that word. Then you will pick one of the four words and say it as you toss the beanbag to someone else.

- Play the game until everyone gets an opportunity to share at least once.

- **Say:** We'll play the game again. This time, when you catch the beanbag, you'll tell us how you can live out that word in your life. For example, if the word were *Peace*, you might say, "I can solve disagreements using words."

- Play the game again, allowing everyone a chance to share at least once.

- **Pray:** God, thank you for your son, Jesus. We remember his birth and celebrate with joy. Help us to remember the joy we feel all year long. Amen.

A Season of Joy

Joseph and Mary had traveled to Bethlehem to register because that was Joseph's hometown. While they were there, Jesus was born. Mary wrapped him in bands of cloth and laid him in a manger.

In a field nearby, shepherds were taking care of their sheep.

God sent an angel to deliver a message to the shepherds. "Do not be afraid! I am here to tell you good news! A baby who is the Savior has been born in Bethlehem. You will find him lying in a manger."

A lot of angels joined the first angel, and they all praised God. "Glory to God! Peace on earth!"

After the angels left the shepherds, the shepherds went to Bethlehem right away and found Mary and Joseph and Jesus. They told them what the angel had said.

The shepherds returned to their fields, glorifying and praising God. Everything had happened just as they had been told.

Based on Luke 2:8-20

Life as a Shepherd in Bible Times

Being a shepherd in Jesus' day was hard work.

Shepherds spent most of their time outside watching their flocks. They had to move the animals around in search of food.

Shepherds often slept outside near their flock to protect it from robbers and wild animals.

A flock usually included of both sheep and goats.

Other members of society often looked down upon shepherds.

Many people considered shepherds to be dishonest.

God chose the shepherds to be the first to receive the news of Jesus' birth even though they were considered dishonest. God's gift of Jesus is for everybody. That's good news!